I0792084

About the author:

Hi! My name is Hailee Walker. I am 21 and I was born in Portland, ME.
I have grown up in a different situation than most.
My experiences are very different. I really want to share my experiences so everyone around who is suffering in silence knows that they aren't alone. Everyone experiences hardships. My poetry is here to help you not feel alone. To help you cope. And most importantly, to show you that it's okay.

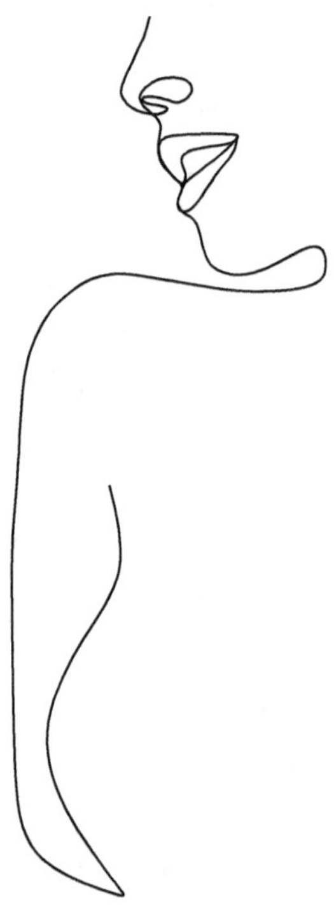

To all of the people out there,
Who are continuing to fight the everyday thought,
"I'm not worth it"
This is for you.

You sit across from me.
With a look on your face.
Questioning, judging, wondering...
Why is she crying.
            And why in front of me.

I sit here.
Hoping you will say something.
Anything.
Please.

Sometimes I pinch myself
because
I pray everything was just a dream.
But really.
It isn't
Because in your dream
you don't
feel pain and enjoy it.

I didn't ask.
I didn't ask to be hit.
I didn't ask to be broken.

Why did you scream at me? Why did you smack me?

It's okay...
It'll get better.

I didn't ask to be loved.
I just hoped.
I didn't beg you to answer me. I didn't ask to be cheated on..

Why did you go?
Why did you go?
Please. Stay.

Sometimes,
My head is under the water.
Sometimes,
My cup is overflowing.
And sometimes,
On purpose,
I hold my breath.
Not to die...
But to remind myself,
I'm still alive.
To remind myself.
And to just...
Feel,
Something.

You sit in the bedroom.
Blade in hand.
Questioning,
Why?
Why do I have to feel this way?

I just want to be...
            Normal.

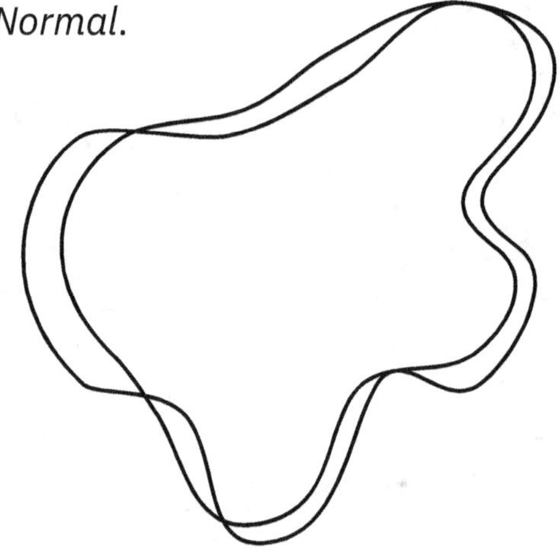

I pray.
Pray you don't come back.
I pray.
I pray.
Pray you don't come back.
I pray.
I pray.
Pray you come back.
I pray.
I pray.
Pray you come back.
I pray.

It's the never ending cycle of abuse.

When you are a child,
And all you see is hate.
You start to learn that love is out of hatred.

Keep your enemies close...
Right?

Some people ask me.
But I refuse to answer.

Because you just don't get it.
No.
I don't love to
hurt myself.

But when all you were *taught*
was that you *deserve* to hurt,
It becomes...
Addicting.
And then you can't stop.

All   I've   seen   is
drugs. *Drugs.*
Abuse.
Abuse.
Drugs.

Ugh.
Sometimes...
I just want to follow the same habits.
        But not because *I want* to do *them.*
I just want to be *understood* by them.
To give me something to relate to.
Something that we could *connect* on.

But why?
Why can't we just connect like family does?

The scars.
Scars are fading.
So it wasn't worth it?
But I need to know it was for something.
Please.
Please don't go.

Cause when you go... then no one will know
The story.
My story.

I don't do it for you.
I do it for me.
For something.
Something to feel. Please.
Dont.
Go.

There isn't enough prayers,
Finger crosses,
Or birthday wishes...

To wish away this pain. This bottle
inside of me. This emptiness.
            That's full.

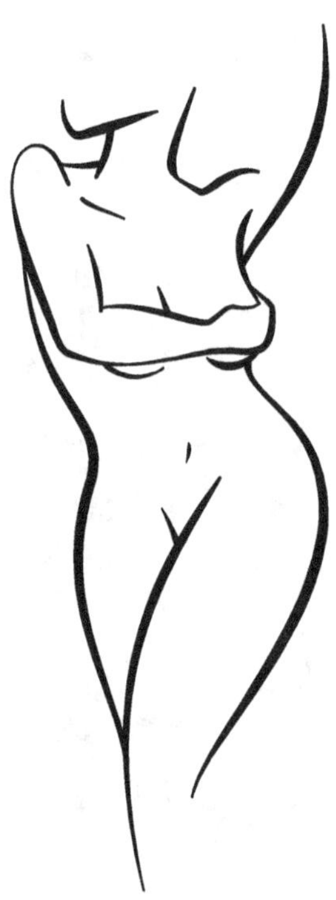

I just want to be held.
Without being
forced to do anything.
3x.
Why is this becoming
a normal thing in children.
Why do I have to
beg for someone to stop.

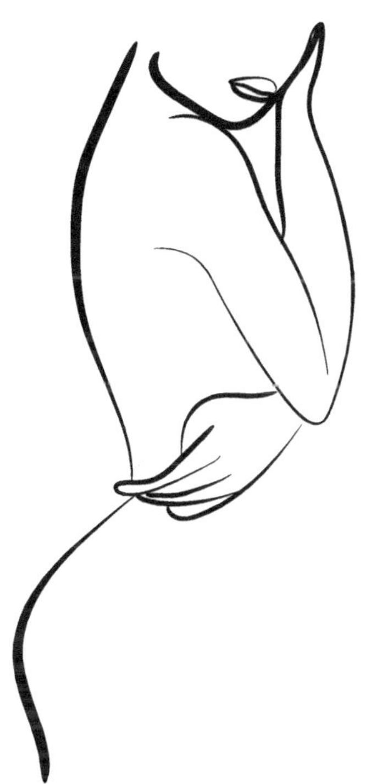

My notes app.
Holds something.
Something about everything.

Yet I still come running back.

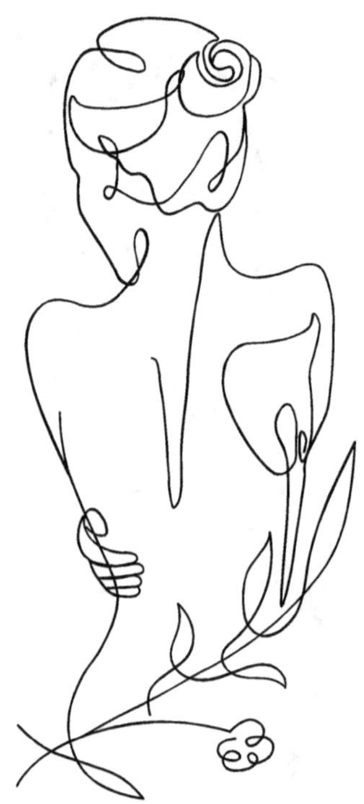

The more you scream.
The more I stay.
The more the promises are broken.
The more I stay.
The more abuse there is.
The more I stay.

I'll never go.

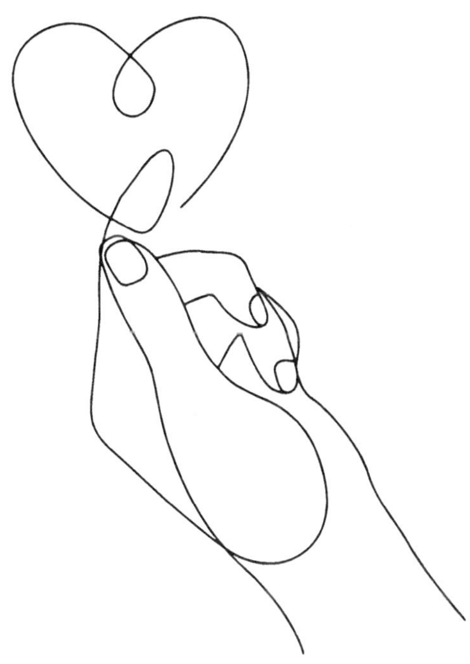

My therapist asks me... why do you stay?
Because.
No one will understand.
Why my body has become a cutting board.
                    has self inflicted scars.

has these marks.

Burns.
Cuts.
Bruises.
No one will get it.

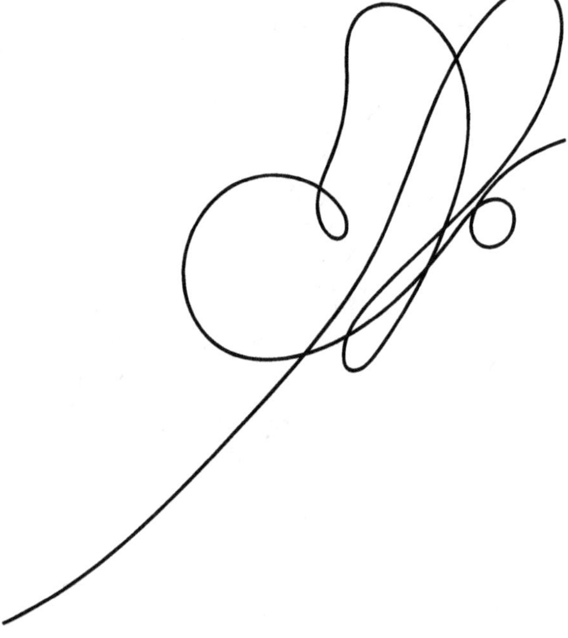

I have no purpose in life anymore
I don't wanna be here
Everyone hates me
And no one gives a fuck about me
I hate myself so much

My goodbye letter:

I'm sorry for not telling anyone.
However I did give the signs.
Everyone knew.

I'm sorry to whoever has to find
me. It's no one's fault.
I didn't want to carry on.

I didn't want to have to beg to be loved.
I didn't want to have to explain myself anymore.

I just wanted to be loved. I
just wanted to feel okay.

No pills, no meds, no therapist could make me okay.

There has been enough damage.
It's no one's fault.
Please just take care of each other.

Make sure Nugget's okay.
Please.
I'm sorry.

When you find me.
Don't go through my phone.
It won't help.
There are secrets
no one knows about.
Not even my therapist.

I sit in these paper scrubs.
How the hell didn't it work.
My next plan was going to be better.

I'm transferred to another place.
Searched.
Head to toe.

Bend over. Cough.

Touched.

I just want to sleep.
I just didn't want to wake up.

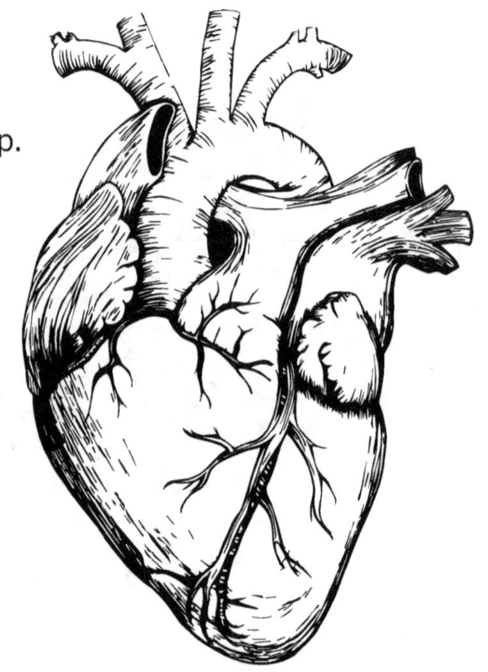

Sometimes I take baths.
Not to bathe.
But to be able to burn
my skin
from how hot the water is.
To be able to hold my breath.
To just fucking
feel
Something.

The day you handed me a
knife and told me to just do it.
Said I was a pussy.

        While my sister watched.
Was the day
I realized you
weren't who everyone
said you were.

How are masks at the store $14.95?
But the mask I beg you to take off,
when we are with people...
is free.
How is it the masks you want to be gone so badly,
so easy to come and go.
How is it the mask I have created from this,
the most expensive mask
anyone will ever know.
The mask I now put on,
is worth $20,000.00.
It works so well.
Even the doctors are fooled.
Want to borrow it?
So you can too.
Let me know,
Careful,
it will fool
you too.

The blood drips on the floor.
Love,
Hatred,
Anxiety,
Depression,
Fear,
Everything,
At that moment.
Is gone.

Why do I do it? This is why.

They never tell you when it will be okay.
They never have answers of when.
We can track time,
track pregnancies,
track death.
Then tell me why,
You doctor.
Can't tell me when it'll finally happen.
Be okay.

My headphones don't block the right things.
The sound in the car only goes to 40.
The sound on my phone isn't high enough.
FUCK.
I just need to shut my mind off.

I'm jealous.
Jealous that your fingers are smooth.
Your wrists are clean.
Your mind is normal.
I'm jealous.
The fact your dad actually wanted to be there.
The fact you didn't have to experience so much narcissism,
that the doctors aren't questioning BPD.
I'm jealous.
That you don't have to meet certain grades.
I'm jealous that you don't flinch
when someone fake hits you.
I'm jealous of you
for not being abused.

I question if it is normal.
Normal to flinch when someone fakes hit me.
Normal to shake when someone yells.
Normal to listen better when being yelled at.
Normal to stay with someone so bad.
Normal to continue to love someone who hurts you so badly.
Normal to pray they don't go but beg for them to leave.
Normal to.
Normal.
Just.
Normal.

You hit me.
I cry.
Wipe the tears.
Then lie.
You smack me.
I cry.
Wipe the tears.
Then lie.
You yell at me.
I cry.
Wipe the tears.
Then lie.
You push me.
I cry.
Wipe the tears.
Then lie.
You cheat on me.
I cry.
Wipe the tears.
Then lie.

I lie to myself.
Tell myself this didn't happen.
It's like someone puts a boulder.
Right on top of
my memory.
But then it reminds
me when it gets bad again.

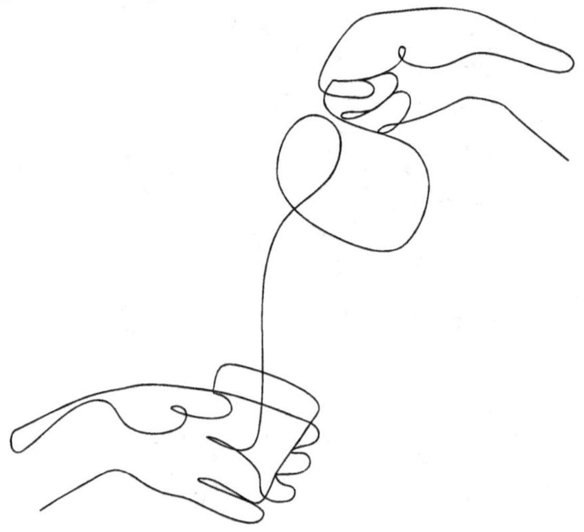

I tell myself it's okay.
Okay to be addicted.
To be addicted to the bad.
All I was shown was to love
the worst people who hate you the most.

I hunch over the toilet.
Puking.
Sticking my fingers as far as they will go.
I am not worthy of food.
I don't deserve to eat.
Just like you said.

Nothing is coming up.
Just tears.
Burning down my face.
Scratching my fingers
covered in bile.

Track.
Starve.
Rice cakes.
Purge.

Oh,
I'm not hungry.
Thank you but I am not hungry.
Oh,
I'm not hungry.
Thank you but I am not hungry.
Oh,
I'm not hungry.
Thank you but I am not hungry.
Oh,
I'm not hungry.
Thank you but I am not hungry.
Oh,
I'm not hungry.
Thank you but I am not hungry.

It's euphoric,
The feeling of not eating.
The feeling of puking up the last bit of anything.
It's euphoric,
Hearing people compliment you.
Finally,
You have succeeded.
Just kidding.
There is never an end.
It will,
Keep,
going.

Being someone,
Considered obese.
But struggling with anorexia and bulimia,
Is the hardest fucking
thing in the world.
Doctors tell me.
        Just stop eating,
         oh you probably binge,
         oh you eat too much.
But really,
My body is getting
to the point of saving
every last piece I eat.
It saves everything now.
And I'm screaming
FUCK YOU.

How do you tell someone,
It's getting bad again.
How do you say these four words?
How do you just say them?
Someone tell me how to keep
the anxiety and fear off their face.
Their disappointment.
Their avoidance.
The looks.
The judgment.
Everything.

I never meant to start a war.
I just wanted to be accepted
by those who were
"supposed" to
love me.

Tears roll,
Down my eyelashes,
Down my cheeks,
Down my chin,
Off my jaw.
They hit my collarbone,
Then my shirt.
At this point the
shirt is now
red, not pink.

Zoning out.
It is my normal day to day thing.
Twirling my hair.
It is my normal day to day thing.
Picking my fingers.
It is my normal day to day thing.
Racing thoughts.
It is my normal day to day thing.

I am listening,
just trying to
shut off everything else.

I can't help but cry.
Cry these tears while I drive.
Seeing swervy lines.
The lights look like haylows.
The breaks look like dots.
I can't help but cry.

After trying so many brands,
You would think one would work.
Nope.
Still nothing,
Nothing can silence the
memories.
The past.
The future.
Or the present.

The system is fucked.
Even after trying to end your life.
You are smacked in the face with a
$3,000.00 bill.
After insurance.
How can you do this?
Especially, to someone
who didn't even
want to be here.
The system is fucked.

The Scars on my Wrist
tell my story.
They are vertical and horizontal.
From the experiences
I have had.
The distances
I have traveled.
The hardships
I have been given.

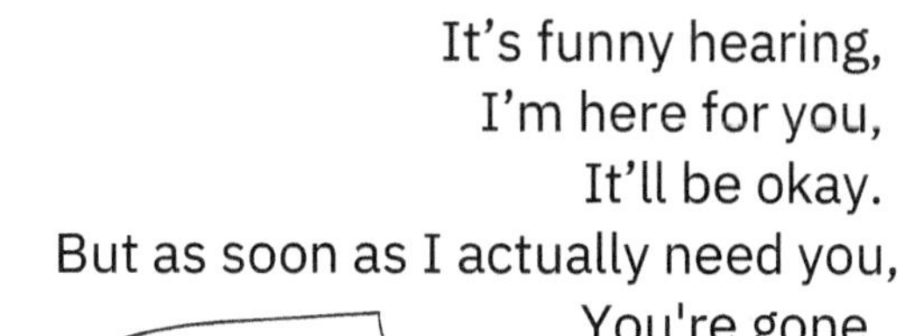

It's funny hearing,
I'm here for you,
It'll be okay.
But as soon as I actually need you,
You're gone.

I'm not sure what is worse.
Having to lie
like you are okay.
Or begging them from the inside
to ask what happened.

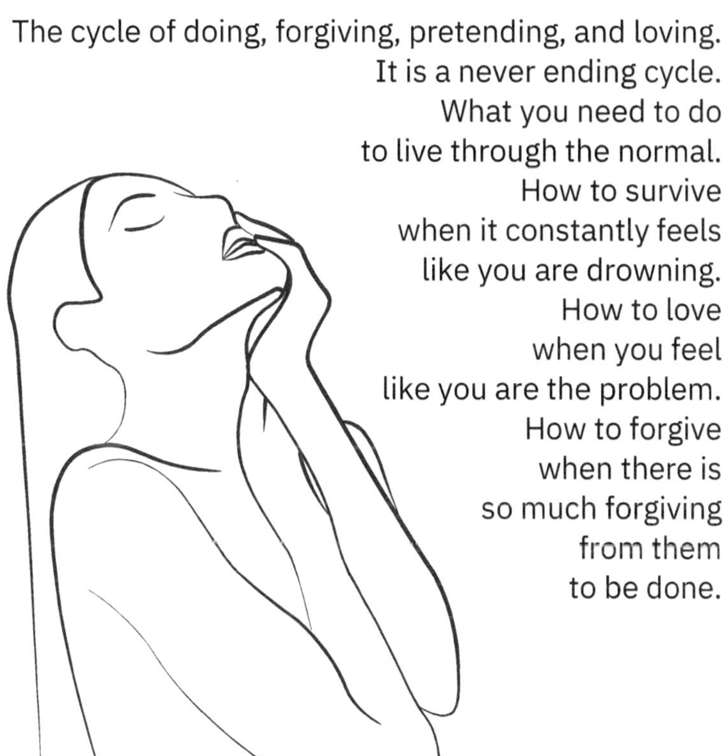

The cycle of doing, forgiving, pretending, and loving.
It is a never ending cycle.
What you need to do
to live through the normal.
How to survive
when it constantly feels
like you are drowning.
How to love
when you feel
like you are the problem.
How to forgive
when there is
so much forgiving
from them
to be done.

I feel like I'm drowning.
Like the water is so high.
It's boiling. Burning. Suffocating.
Please.
Why won't anyone around me
pull the plug to drain this tub.
Why won't anyone around me
grab me and pull me out.
Why won't anyone around me
help me.

I met a guy.
He was older.
I didn't understand why my family didn't approve.
He begged me to leave.
I wanted to stay.
To fix the one who took me away.
Away from the abuse.
The lies.
The tears.
The masks.
I met a guy.
He is older.
I don't understand why my family doesn't approve.
He begs me to stay.
I want to stay.
He's the one who took me away.
Away from the abuse.
The lies.
The tears.
The masks.
I met a guy.

I think about the way he looks at me and I pray.
I think about the feeling of him leaving me and I pray.

Hopes and wishes that he will stay...
or even choose me one day; I pray.
Finally, hours on end.
I'm with my best friend and I pray.

To my nana up above watching me, I pray.
Listening to my family's comments, I pray.

Hope and tears that this could be taken from me, I pray.
Trying everyday to help him get better and love himself; and
for one day he will realize it's not his fault. I pray.

Grabbing onto the last hope there is, I pray.

Hearing my dad bash him, I pray.

The feeling of stomach knotting, squeezing, and crying. I pray.
Pray that he won't go.
Pray that he stays.
Pray that this will be a forever thing.
Pray that I get to wake up,
but in his arms.
Pray that someone won't ruin this. I pray.
The reassurance when he tells me, you don't need to pray;
I'm not going anywhere. I pray.

Never ever having the right amount of security, is the
reason... I pray.
Never believing and always being taught I'm not enough.
Or that everything is my fault... I'm sorry; I pray.

So when someone tells me or looks at me strange, I pray.

I pray they will find the love I get.
The feeling of warmth he gives.
The security and hope that is brought.
I pray they will get to understand why I pray for him to stay.
For people to let it be.
For the crooked faces and stairs to change.
For the acceptance that I don't get; and the constant worry of
what am I doing wrong.
I pray.

I pray, for my dad to love me the way he loves my
sister. For him to accept me the way he does to her.
But if I don't get it; I keep praying.

I will be okay because I pray.
I pray that the prayers that have worked; continue.
I will pray for him to keep being him.
I pray the love continues to grow and we grow together.
I pray for everyone watching.
I pray he knows how loved he is and how much he's fixed me.

I pray.